The Fruit of the Spirit

A Practical Guide to Discerning the Spirit of God

By Glenn Tabor

A Publication of:
Get In The Bible Ministries

VA

Vabella Publishing

Vabella Publishing
P.O. Box 1052
Carrollton, Georgia 30112

A Publication of:
Get In The Bible Ministries
PO Box 486
Winston, GA 30187
www.getinthebible.org

All Scripture quotations are taken from the King James Version of the Holy Bible.

Cover designed by Glenn and Elesha Tabor

Printed in the United States of America

ISBN 978-1-938230-85-1

LCCN 2014919952

10 9 8 7 6 5 4 3 2 1

Table of Contents

Foreword

I am honored to write this foreword for Brother Glenn Tabor's book, <u>The Fruit of the Spirit</u>. The subtitle, "A Practical Guide to Discerning the Spirit of God" is very appropriate. Glenn is one of the most practical people I know. Everything he does is well thought out. He builds his Bible study "line upon line, precept upon precept" in the same way he orders his daily life.

Glenn's desire is to help his readers build a solid Scriptural foundation for their lives. In the Sermon on the Mount, Jesus said those who hear His words and do them are like a man who digs deep to build the foundation of his house upon a rock. When the storms come, and they will come, that house will stand.

I love Glenn's subject. The Fruit of the Spirit is available to every Christian. Our lives can be filled with it when we allow the Holy Spirit to control us. And who doesn't want more love, joy, and peace; who couldn't use more long-suffering and gentleness; who wouldn't be a better Christian with more goodness and faith in their life; and who wouldn't benefit from more meekness and temperance.

I trust this book will further your knowledge and understanding of the nine fold Fruit of the Spirit, and that this understanding will lead you to seek the filling of the Holy Spirit day by day.

Dr. W. Kenneth Johns

Introduction

But the fruit of the Spirit is love,

joy, peace, longsuffering,

gentleness, goodness, faith,

Meekness, temperance:

against such there is no law.

Galatians 5:22-23

These two verses may seem simple. They have been taught to children in Sunday School for generations. We teach them using a tree and cardboard cutouts of apples and bananas. We have our children memorize them. These seemingly simple verses are often overlooked by our adult minds because they have been used for so long to entertain the children. But locked in these two lines of scripture there is a wealth of information to take with us in our daily walk with God. These verses will be our jumping off point for learning to discern the Spirit of God...

At one time or another we have all had a question about knowing the Spirit of God in our lives and how we can KNOW the difference between what is God's voice prompting us and the influence of the spirit of the world or our own flesh enticing us into something.

We are told to try the spirits...

> Beloved, believe not every spirit, but try the spirits whether they are of God: because many false prophets are gone out into the world. Hereby know ye the Spirit of God: Every spirit that confesseth that Jesus Christ is come in the flesh is of God: And every spirit that confesseth not that Jesus Christ is come in the flesh is not of God: and this is that spirit of antichrist, whereof ye have heard that it should come; and even now already is it in the world.
> 1 John 4:1-3

But these verses about confessing Christ in the flesh are meant to help us determine who is a brother and who is not. Anyone who denies that Christ is come in the flesh of not of God. This alone is not enough to determine whether something is of the Spirit of God. Because, you see, even the devils know the name of Jesus.

> Thou believest that there is one God; thou doest well: the **devils also believe, and tremble**.
> James 2:19

And when he was come to the other side into

the country of the Gergesenes, there met him two possessed with devils, coming out of the tombs, exceeding fierce, so that no man might pass by that way. And, behold, they cried out, saying, **What have we to do with thee, Jesus, thou Son of God**? art thou come hither to torment us before the time?
Matthew 8:28-29

We see from these verses, that even the devils can recognize Jesus as the Son of God. They may tremble at the mention of His name, but they still call Him by name. These are the crafty ones that we definitely need to be on guard for. Those that outright deny Christ are easy to spot. However, it is the spirits that know who God is and know the name of His Son, but deny their authority that are the most dangerous. These are the spirits that are at work in the world causing countless brothers and sisters in Christ to go astray and countless more to never know Christ at all. These are the powers that we truly need to be concerned with. There **must** be some way we can know the difference in this world where "we wrestle not against flesh and blood, but against principalities, against powers, against the rulers of the darkness of this world, against spiritual wickedness in high places." (Ephesians 6:12)

From whence come wars and fightings among you? come they not hence, **even of your lusts that war in your members?**
James 4:1

For though we walk in the flesh, **we do not war after the flesh**: (**For the weapons**

of our warfare are not carnal, but mighty through God to the pulling down of strong holds;) Casting down imaginations, and every high thing that exalteth itself against the knowledge of God, and **bringing into captivity every thought to the obedience of Christ**; And having in a readiness to revenge all disobedience, when your obedience is fulfilled.
2 Corinthians 10:3-6

This charge I commit unto thee, son Timothy, according to the prophecies which went before on thee, **that thou by them mightest war a good warfare**;
1 Timothy 1:18

Spiritual warfare is very real. It is not a battle of strength and might and weapons of the flesh. It is not a tangible fight for physical dominion. It is a war between the spirit of worldliness and the Spirit of Righteousness dwelling in the believer. This war is over the minds and hearts of men, either to keep them from ever knowing Christ and His gift of redemption, or drawing a person far enough away from God that they are ineffective in their Christian walk. Many books have been written on the aspects and weapons of spiritual warfare, so we will not elaborate on that right now. Just keep in your mind that spiritual warfare is real, and it is a war that is waged daily in the hearts and minds of every Christian. Paul summed it up best in this phrase, "I die daily," indicating that he had to mortify (or kill) his flesh daily and bring himself into subjection to the will of God for his life. The battle only begins at salvation... it is far from over.

The need for a means to discern the Spirit of God in a practical and daily applicable way is obvious. This is such an important question that it cannot be ignored or dismissed as some thing that we cannot know for sure. You see, the important things of the Bible... things like the plan of salvation, the love of God, our eternity with Him or eternal punishment, even judgment... these things are simple to understand. Simple enough that a child can grasp the concepts well enough to know they need a Savior. The same is true for discerning the Spirit of God. We have over-complicated what God has set forth in His Book, and confused it to the point that no one seems to know for sure. It is my hope that this book illustrates how easy it is to discern the will of God and to know if something is of God or not. Our approach to this question can be summed up in the verses from 1st Corinthians.

> For what man knoweth the things of a man, save the spirit of man which is in him? even so **the things of God knoweth no man, but the Spirit of God.** Now we have received, not the spirit of the world, **but the spirit which is of God; that we might know the things that are freely given to us of God.** Which things also we speak, not in the words which man's wisdom teacheth, but **which the Holy Ghost teacheth; comparing spiritual things with spiritual.** But the natural man receiveth not the things of the Spirit of God: for they are foolishness unto him: neither can he know them, because **they are spiritually discerned.**
> 1 Corinthians 2:11-14

The necessary things of God are simple and freely given. These things are taught by His Spirit, and we can see these things in His Word by comparing spiritual things (His Word) with spiritual things (His Word). So lets approach the question, how can we know the difference between the Spirit of God and the spirit of man or the spirits of this world?

It is not that hard!

> And God said, Let the earth bring forth grass, the herb yielding seed, and **the fruit tree yielding fruit after his kind, whose seed is in itself, upon the earth: and it was so**. And the earth brought forth grass, and herb yielding seed after his kind, and the tree yielding fruit, whose seed was in itself, after his kind: and God saw that it was good.
> Genesis 1:11-12

This may seem like a strange place to start, but God has set forth a universal concept. From the beginning, trees have yielded fruit after its kind. Christ reiterates this for us.

> Ye shall know them by their fruits. Do men gather grapes of thorns, or figs of thistles? Even so every good tree bringeth forth good fruit; but a corrupt tree bringeth forth evil fruit. A good tree cannot bring forth evil fruit, neither can a corrupt tree bring forth good fruit. Every tree that bringeth not forth good fruit is hewn down, and cast into the fire. **Wherefore by their fruits ye shall know them**.
> Matthew 7:16-20

You will know the tree by the fruit it bares. This doesn't only apply to false prophets and Pharisees, but it also applies to those who call themselves Christians. God uses this same principle to help us discern between the spirit of the flesh and the Spirit of God. Very simply, we know if it is of the Spirit of God if it produces the fruit of the Spirit. Just as we know a tree by the fruit it bares, or men by the fruit they bare, we can know the Spirit of God, by the fruit it bares. A good tree CANNOT bring forth evil fruit, and a corrupt tree CANNOT bring forth good fruit. And God in His wisdom has set down these fruit for us, so we do not have to guess at what is meant by the term fruit, or make things up to fill the gaps in our understanding. These are the fruit of the Spirit.

> But the fruit of the Spirit is **love, joy, peace, longsuffering, gentleness, goodness, faith, Meekness, temperance:** against such there is no law.
> Galatians 5:22-23

We will see in this study how the fruit of the Spirit covers every aspect of our human relations and every facet of our Christian walk. It is not just a list of "good ideas", but a comprehensive list of what we should be looking for if we are in doubt of God's presence or influence in a certain situation. They are the criteria that we can use for every situation to KNOW that we are hearing the influence of God and **not** the influences of this world or our own wayward hearts that all so often drown out His still small voice.

Part 1
Understanding Fruit

Before we can explore the fruit of the Spirit, we must first understand a few things about fruit.

When we talk about the "fruit" that something bares, we are talking about what it produces... it's product, or work. People produce good fruit in the form of acts of kindness and Christian behavior, or evil fruit in the form of maliciousness or hurtful or destructive behavior. Just as in the verses we read earlier.

> Ye shall know them by their fruits. Do men gather grapes of thorns, or figs of thistles? Even so **every good tree bringeth forth good fruit**; but **a corrupt tree bringeth forth evil fruit**. A good tree cannot bring forth evil fruit, neither can a corrupt tree bring forth good fruit. Every tree that bringeth not forth good fruit is hewn down, and cast into the fire. Wherefore by their fruits ye shall know them.
> Matthew 7:16-20

The first and possibly least understood aspect of fruit is that the fruit of the tree does not feed the tree. Just as our works (by which our faith is exemplified) produce for others, not for ourselves. An apple tree does not produce apples for itself. It produces apples for those that feed from the tree. Our fruit is likewise. We do not feed ourselves with our fruit... we feed others. If our works are done to further ourselves, bring praise or prestige to ourselves, to edify us, to let our voice be heard, we have our reward....just as it tells us in Matthew.

Take heed that ye do not your alms before men, to be seen of them: otherwise ye have no reward of your Father which is in heaven. Therefore when thou doest thine alms, **do not sound a trumpet before thee, as the hypocrites do in the synagogues and in the streets, that they may have glory of men. Verily I say unto you, They have their reward.** But when thou doest alms, let not thy left hand know what thy right hand doeth: That thine alms may be in secret: and thy Father which seeth in secret himself shall reward thee openly. And when thou prayest, **thou shalt not be as the hypocrites are: for they love to pray standing in the synagogues and in the corners of the streets, that they may be seen of men. Verily I say unto you, They have their reward.** But thou, when thou prayest, enter into thy closet, and when thou hast shut thy door, pray to thy Father which is in secret; and thy Father which seeth in secret shall reward thee openly. But when ye pray, use not vain repetitions, as the heathen do: for they think that they shall be heard for their much speaking. Be not ye therefore like unto them: for your Father knoweth what things ye have need of, before ye ask him.
Matthew 6:1-8

Christ is telling us that if we do something for the recognition of having done it... that is all the reward we get. That is all the fruit it is going to produce. So, just as we produce fruit for those around us to help sustain and support and edify them... the

Spirit of God, produces fruit within us to help sustain and support and edify us. This concept lends itself well to the fact that the Spirit does not testify of itself. We see this in the words of Jesus in the Gospel of John:

> Howbeit when he, the Spirit of truth, is come, he will guide you into all truth: **for he shall not speak of himself**; but whatsoever he shall hear, that shall he speak: and he will shew you things to come. John 16:13

When the Spirit testifies it speaks of God and of Christ, but it does not edify itself. Else, as Christ has set forth, there would be no reward. The Spirit could not bare fruit in our lives if it edified itself. So the first concept of fruit that we must grasp is that the tree does not produce fruit to sustain or edify itself.

We can see this in action in our own experiences. Many have done grand gestures of giving or service, possibly even in our lives. Some have done it in the background, wanting not to be seen or heard, and some have done it in the spotlight. The actions and end result may be the same, but for one the intention is to be of service in a quiet and humble way, the other does it to be seen and noticed for their gracious actions. The first does it to edify and strengthen another, which is fruit for another. The other does it for his own edification, which is fruit for himself, thus he has his reward.

The second concept of fruit that I want to point out is that, by definition, fruit bares the seed of the tree for the purpose of reproducing itself. The fruit carries the seed. And just like the parable tells us, not all seeds will sprout.

> A sower went out to sow his seed: and as he sowed, some fell by the way side; and it was trodden down, and the fowls of the air devoured it. And some fell upon a rock; and as soon as it was sprung up, it withered away, because it lacked moisture. And some fell among thorns; and the thorns sprang up with it, and choked it. And other fell on good ground, and sprang up, and bare fruit an hundredfold. And when he had said these things, he cried, He that hath ears to hear, let him hear.
> Luke 8:5-8

And just a few verses later...

> Now the parable is this: **The seed is the word of God.**
> Luke 8:11

There is no great hidden mystery here. This is how our works carry the message of Christ and open the door for us to share the gospel with others. The person is receiving the fruit of our labors, our Christian deeds. But carried with that deed, if it is motivated by Gods love shining through us, is the seed of the Word of God. Some will take hold, some will not... we just need to be sure that our works are carrying the right seeds, meaning that is motivated by the love of God abiding in us, and not our own interests. We can ensure that our works are carrying the right seeds by recognizing the Spirit of God in them.

So we see that fruit (our work) does not sustain the tree that bares it, and that the fruit, by its very nature, carries the seed of the Word of God.

Now, the glory of it all, as I mentioned earlier, is that we do not have to guess as to what are these fruit of the Spirit. The Bible is gracious enough to tell us and save us from our own ignorance and confusion.

> **The fruit of the Spirit is <u>love</u>, <u>joy</u>, <u>peace</u>, <u>longsuffering</u>, <u>gentleness</u>, <u>goodness</u>, <u>faith</u>, <u>meekness</u>, <u>temperance</u>: against such there is no law.**

We will be examining each of these fruit individually, and see how they apply to our lives in a practical and effective way. Being aware of how these fruit impact our daily lives, and watching for the evidence of them in our relationships, we can know that we are walking in the way God would have us go.

Part 2
The Fruit of Love

Love is the first fruit, and we could actually stop right there. If you have love... well, I'll just let the Bible tell us...

> Owe no man any thing, but to love one another: for **he that loveth another hath fulfilled the law**. For this, Thou shalt not commit adultery, Thou shalt not kill, Thou shalt not steal, Thou shalt not bear false witness, Thou shalt not covet; and if there be any other commandment, it is briefly comprehended in this saying, namely, Thou shalt love thy neighbour as thyself. Love worketh no ill to his neighbour: **therefore love is the fulfilling of the law.**
> Romans 13:8-10

> For, brethren, ye have been called unto liberty; only use not liberty for an occasion to the flesh, but by love serve one another. **For all the law is fulfilled in one word, even in this; Thou shalt love thy neighbour as thyself.**
> Galatians 5:13-14

> If ye **fulfil the royal law according to the scripture**, Thou shalt love thy neighbour as thyself, ye do well:
> James 2:8

That is three witnesses from scripture telling us that love toward one another is the fulfillment of the law. And as it has already told us in Galatians 5... there is no law against these fruit of the Spirit. Part of the perfection of God's Word is evidenced here. **The law is satisfied by something the law has no power to control.**

21

It was through this law satisfying love that God made a way for us to come unto Him.

> For God **so loved** the world, that he gave his only begotten Son, that whosoever believeth in him should not perish, but have everlasting life.
> John 3:16

So, if we love one another with that kind of law satisfying love, we fulfill the law and thus satisfy all the fruit of the Spirit.   Which would mean God living in us (because God is love as set forth in 1st John 4), having Him sitting on the throne of our hearts, and living in humble obedience to His reign, having our thoughts and actions focused on bringing glory and honor to Him... we could stop there at the first fruit of love. Not only that, but when we look at what is said about Charity the counter part of love we see that all other types of fruit are represented.

> Though I speak with the tongues of men and of angels, and have not charity, I am become as sounding brass, or a tinkling cymbal. And though I have the gift of prophecy, and understand all mysteries, and all knowledge; and though I have all faith, so that I could remove mountains, and have not charity, I am nothing. And though I bestow all my goods to feed the poor, and though I give my body to be burned, and have not charity, it profiteth me nothing. Charity **suffereth long (long suffering)**, and is **kind (goodness)**; charity envieth not; **charity**

vaunteth not itself, is not puffed up (meekness), Doth not behave itself unseemly (gentleness), seeketh not her own (this is also an aspect of meekness), is not easily provoked (temperance), thinketh no evil (peace); Rejoiceth not in iniquity, but **rejoiceth in the truth (joy)**; Beareth all things, believeth all things, hopeth all things, endureth all things. **Charity never faileth (Faith, because we know that faith abideth forever):** but whether there be prophecies, they shall fail; whether there be tongues, they shall cease; whether there be knowledge, it shall vanish away. For we know in part, and we prophesy in part. But when that which is perfect is come, then that which is in part shall be done away. When I was a child, I spake as a child, I understood as a child, I thought as a child: but when I became a man, I put away childish things. For now we see through a glass, darkly; but then face to face: now I know in part; but then shall I know even as also I am known. **And now abideth faith, hope, charity,** these three; but the greatest of these is charity.

1 Corinthians 13:1-13
(Parenthesis added)

Through love for one another (lost or otherwise), we fulfill all the law. In love we satisfy all aspects of the fruit of the Spirit. There are nine fruit listed, but the remaining eight are manifestations or facets of the first fruit which is Love. We will take a look at each of these remaining fruit and see how each one applies specifically to a different aspect of our Christian walk.

There is definitely a connection between love and charity, but they are not exactly the same thing. There is a reason that these two words, often synonymous in scripture, are used at different times. Love is what we **feel**. The emotion or compassion we have for another. Charity is what we **do** in response to that compassion. We can see a similar distinction reflected in these few verses from James talking about the difference between faith and works.

> What doth it profit, my brethren, though a man say he hath faith, and have not works? can faith save him? If a brother or sister be naked, and destitute of daily food, And one of you say unto them, **Depart in peace, be ye warmed and filled**; notwithstanding **ye give them not those things which are needful to the body**; what doth it profit? **Even so faith, if it hath not works, is dead, being alone.**
> James 2:14-17

Lets take another look at the verses we just saw in 1st Corinthians concerning Charity.

> Though I speak with the tongues of men and of angels, **and have not charity, I am become as sounding brass, or a tinkling cymbal.** And though I have the gift of prophecy, and understand all mysteries, and all knowledge; and though I have all faith, so that I could remove

mountains, and **have not charity, I am nothing**. And though I bestow all my goods to feed the poor, and though I give my body to be burned, and **have not charity, it profiteth me nothing**.

1 Corinthians 13:1-3

You see, recognizing a need and even verbally acknowledging a need you see in another is worthless if it is alone. Regardless of how bad you feel for the person or how much it pulls at your heart strings, it is worthless unless you are willing to act on that need. I can feel bad all day about the fact that you are hungry, but if I never take action to change that, all of my compassion and love for you in your situation is of no use. The flip side of that is even though you do great acts of kindness or compassion, if they are done without Godly love being the motivation behind it, they are profitless. It is a two part system, we must have **faith** which is reflected in our **works** (it is lifeless without them)... and we must have **love** for others, which is exemplified in our acts of **charity**.

Compassion or love for another alone is dead because it bares no fruit... again, love is what we feel, but that love is not quick (lively) without the charity (the actions we do) that put that love in motion.

I will say it again... The first fruit of the Spirit, which is love, is all-encompassing. Remember, it is not just the warm feelings that we feel, or the compassion we have for another, but also the manifestation of our love through our acts of charity that is the fruit. We have also seen that the tree does not profit from its own fruit, but the fruit profits others. People do not gain blessings from us feeling love for them, they are blessed by the actions that love causes us to do.

So when we are doing our acts of charity, we must ask ourselves if we are being motivated by a Godly love and compassion for the person, or are we doing them to satisfy ourselves and bring honour to ourselves.

Before we move on there is a peculiar thing about these verses in Galatians 5 that I want to point out. Lets take another quick look.

> **22 But the fruit of the Spirit is love, joy, peace, longsuffering, gentleness, goodness, faith,**
> **23 Meekness, temperance: against such there is no law.**
> **Galatians 5:22-23**

Notice that God has, in His wisdom, set meekness and temperance off by themselves in verse 23. This made me wonder if these are not a linked set. If these are linked somehow, then possibly the others are "sets" that correspond with each other. Once we begin to look at the remaining eight fruit in this fashion, God's word begins to unfold in a way we may have never noticed before.

Part 3
The Fruit of Joy and Peace

At the beginning we said that the fruit of the Spirit cover every aspect of our Christian walk. Love is the foundation upon which all the fruit are established, but God has allowed us these guideposts in the form of the other fruit to help us in every part of our lives. We will see over the next few chapters how these pairs of fruit compliment each other and paint a picture of how God's Spirit is to impact our lives.

Joy and Peace are the first set we see, and they are **how love governs our attitude toward our circumstances.**

When things are good, when we feel God in our lives and feel Him moving through us and blessing us, we rejoice. We feel joy!

> And Zadok the priest took an horn of oil out of the tabernacle, and anointed Solomon. And they blew the trumpet; and all the people said, God save king Solomon. **And all the people came up after him, and the people piped with pipes, and rejoiced with great joy, so that the earth rent with the sound of them.**
> 1 Kings 1:39-40

The Joy of these men celebrating the new king was so loud it sounded like an earthquake.

> Give thanks unto the LORD, call upon his name, make known his deeds among the people. Sing unto him, sing psalms unto him, talk ye of all his wondrous works. Glory ye in his holy name: **let the heart of them rejoice that seek the LORD.**
> 1 Chronicles 16:8-10

This is an example of the quiet rejoicing of the heart... but notice that before the joy of the heart... there was singing.

> But let **all those that put their trust in thee rejoice**: let them **ever shout for joy**, because thou defendest them: **let them also that love thy name be joyful in thee.**
> Psalms 5:11

Shout out your joy forever. Shout the name of the Lord.

These are just a few of the many examples of Joy in the Bible. We rejoice... we feel joy... during the good times... during the times we feel God near us. This joy is not quiet. I'm not saying that we should be jumping and hollering all the day long, but there is a time to praise and honor Him and let Him know that you are there and recognize what He has done for you. There is also a time to tell others. This aspect of the fruit is manifested in the joy we feel for the Lord being in our lives, and we are to announce this joy. We cannot depend on our actions alone to speak of Christ in us. We MUST be willing to speak His name and explain the reason for our hope, and the motivation behind our actions.

> And **hope maketh not ashamed**; because the love of God is shed abroad in our hearts by the Holy Ghost which is given unto us.
> Romans 5:5

Joy is what we feel about our life circumstance when things are good, and this joy is expressed in our praises to God. But when things are hard... the loss of a loved one, the loss of employment, financial or family problems... that is when we find peace in Jesus.

> **Grace and peace be multiplied unto you** through the knowledge of God, and of Jesus our Lord, According as his divine power hath given unto us all things that pertain unto life and godliness, through the knowledge of him that hath called us to glory and virtue: **Whereby are given unto us exceeding great and precious promises**: that by these ye might be partakers of the divine nature, having escaped the corruption that is in the world through lust.
> 2 Peter 1:2-4

Peace be multiplied unto you, not because you will not suffer, but because of the promises that are made to you by your Redeemer.

> Peace I leave with you, my peace I give unto you: not as the world giveth, give I unto you. Let not your heart be troubled, neither let it be afraid.
> John 14:27

This is a peace that only Christ can bring into a persons life. It is His peace that He gives. The world cannot offer anything that comes close. We should feel this peace, not only in times of trouble or persecution, but also in times of fear. Take a

31

look at these instances where peace is declared in the face of fear. We start with Joseph talking with his brothers.

> And he said, **Peace be to you, fear not**: your God, and the God of your father, hath given you treasure in your sacks: I had your money. And he brought Simeon out unto them.
> Genesis 43:23

Or the Lord talking to Gideon.

> And the LORD said unto him, **Peace be unto thee; fear not**: thou shalt not die.
> Judges 6:23

Or again, the Lord talking to Daniel.

> And said, O man greatly beloved, **fear not: peace be unto thee,** be strong, yea, be strong. And when he had spoken unto me, I was strengthened, and said, Let my lord speak; for thou hast strengthened me.
> Daniel 10:19

And finally, the Christ Himself talking to the disciples.

> Then the same day at evening, being the first day of the week, when the doors were shut where **the disciples were assembled for fear of the Jews**, came **Jesus and stood in the midst, and saith unto them, Peace be unto you.**
> John 20:19

Peace is the Biblical response to fear. I want to share with you a few examples of this peace. The verse above from John is most telling in that they did not fear Jesus, but they were in hiding for fear of the Jews. They feared what was outside the door of their upper room. We can see the fruit of Peace manifested in our lives when we are in those times of loss and trouble and fear, and know, not just hope but **know**, that God is there with us.

Here are a few examples of what Biblical peace looks like.

Stephen as he is being stoned:
And cast him out of the city, and stoned him: and the witnesses laid down their clothes at a young man's feet, whose name was Saul. And they stoned Stephen, calling upon God, and saying, **Lord Jesus, receive my spirit**. And he kneeled down, and cried with a loud voice, **Lord, lay not this sin to their charge**. And when he had said this, he fell asleep.
Acts 7:58-60

Stephen could have just as easily cried out in pain and distress, or cursed those that threw rocks at him. But instead, he responded with the peace that Jesus gave him and forgiveness for those that persecuted him.

Paul and Silas in prison:
And when they had laid many stripes upon them, they cast them into prison, charging the jailor to keep them safely: Who, having

received such a charge, thrust them into the inner prison, and made their feet fast in the stocks. **And at midnight Paul and Silas prayed, and sang praises unto God**: and the prisoners heard them. And suddenly there was a great earthquake, so that the foundations of the prison were shaken: and immediately all the doors were opened, and every one's bands were loosed. Acts 16:23-26

Paul and Silas did not meet their circumstances with despair or worry. They had the peace of Jesus with them, and sang and praised the Lord even in jail. When the doors were opened, they did not run. Their fear had already been addressed, so they felt no need to run.

Eli hearing of the fate of his sons:

And the LORD said to Samuel, Behold, I will do a thing in Israel, at which both the ears of every one that heareth it shall tingle. In that day I will perform against Eli all things which I have spoken concerning his house: when I begin, I will also make an end. For I have told him that I will judge his house for ever for the iniquity which he knoweth; because his sons made themselves vile, and he restrained them not. And therefore I have sworn unto the house of Eli, that the iniquity of Eli's house shall not be purged with sacrifice nor offering for ever.

1 Samuel 3:11-14 *(and continuing just a few verse down)*

And Samuel told him every whit, and hid nothing from him. And he said, **It is the LORD: let him do what seemeth him good.**
1 Samuel 3:18

Eli has just heard of the impending death of his sons, and the erasing of his family name from the earth. He did not cry out or curse God, but took it simply as God's will and "let Him do what seemeth good." Even in the bad times we can see the Spirit of God in our lives manifest as the peace of Christ, and praising the Lord. This is Biblical peace.

Joy is the excitement and energy we feel when God is with us and the praises we sing in the good times... but peace is what we are to feel when God is with us in the bad times, in times of fear and trouble. The common thread there is that God is with us in all of these times and He is always worthy of our praise.

In both of these situations, we must be willing to give a reason for our praise and our hope. The world we encounter does not just need to see us rejoice, or see us patiently endure a trouble. They need to know why we can do so. Everyone needs to know Christ, and they cannot know who He is, or what He can do for them if we are silent. When we are rejoicing, and another notices our joy... tell them how Jesus has brought that joy to you and that it can be theirs also. When you are troubled on every side, but not in despair, explain to those looking on at your plight, that you are not alone and you are not forsaken. They need to hear this, so they will know that Christ is the source of your peace.

One more quick note.

> Let not then your good be evil spoken of:
> For the **kingdom of God** is not meat and
> drink; but righteousness, **and peace, and
> joy in the Holy Ghost.**
> Romans 14:16-17

And isn't that what we are talking about... the
kingdom of God is God sitting on the throne of our
hearts and us living in obedience to His reign, and
feeling His Spirit acting in our lives.

We must ask ourselves, when we reflect on our lives
and circumstances, do we have an underlying
attitude of joy? Or is there anger, or resentment, or
"if only this would have happened... or not
happened" then things would be joyful? Better
still, can we share in the joy of the blessings of
others... even if they receive the blessing we think
should have been ours?

When considering our lives in the roughest of
times, times of loss or tribulation, do we feel peace
knowing not only that God is going to pull us
through, but He is right there with us? Are we at
peace with the certain knowledge that ultimately
we will be blessed regardless of the circumstances
in which we find ourselves? Or are we always
crying out "why me Lord?"

These two fruit of the Spirit, joy and peace, are the
hallmarks of the Christian walk. These are what set
those who believe apart from those who do not.

Peace and joy is what the world sees in us that makes the difference. So ask yourself again... do you feel joy and peace when reflecting on your life?

Part 4
The Fruit of Longsuffering and Gentleness

Joy and Peace is how love governs our attitude towards our circumstances (the good and the bad), Longsuffering and Gentleness is **how love governs our attitudes towards those that do not have a relationship with Jesus**... in short, our attitude toward the Lost.

Before we start discussing Longsuffering, I want to take a moment to clarify the difference between suffering and enduring. They are oftentimes used interchangeably, and most of the time it does not matter, but they are not the same thing. In a nut shell, we must endure things we cannot change, but we choose to suffer. We *endure* things like the loss of a loved one, the loss of a limb, or some other life altering event that we cannot change and oftentimes had no control over the outcome. Sometimes we must endure the consequences of our past actions or poor choices, like a criminal history or a bankruptcy. We cannot go back in time and change the fact that certain choices were made or that certain events occurred. Ignoring these things does not make them go away, so we must endure the long term consequences. However, we *suffer* from things that we have the power to change or remove ourselves from, but choose not to. A few examples might be: we suffer with obnoxious in-laws (we can choose not to see them, but to keep peace we suffer through the visit), in some instances we suffer with bad health (we know we can reduce our cholesterol by eating better, but we choose to eat poorly), we may suffer from a bad habit like smoking or playing too many video games. *We suffer through what we allow despite the displeasure it brings us*, and *we endure what we cannot avoid or change*. Longsuffering therefore is allowing that which brings us displeasure for a long period of time.

One of my favorite (and clearest) examples of suffering is seen in Matthew and also reiterated in Mark and Luke.

> Then were there brought unto him little children, that he should put his hands on them, and pray: and **the disciples rebuked them**. But Jesus said, **Suffer little children, and forbid them not, to come unto me**: for of such is the kingdom of heaven. And he laid his hands on them, and departed thence.
> Matthew 19:13-15

> And they brought young children to him, that he should touch them: **and his disciples rebuked those that brought them**. But when Jesus saw it, he was much displeased, and said unto them, **Suffer the little children to come unto me, and forbid them not**: for of such is the kingdom of God. Verily I say unto you, Whosoever shall not receive the kingdom of God as a little child, he shall not enter therein. And he took them up in his arms, put his hands upon them, and blessed them.
> Mark 10:13-16

> And they brought unto him also infants, that he would touch them: **but when his disciples saw it, they rebuked them**. But Jesus called them unto him, and said, **Suffer little children to come unto me,**

and forbid them not: for of such is the kingdom of God. Verily I say unto you, Whosoever shall not receive the kingdom of God as a little child shall in no wise enter therein.
Luke 18:15-17

The disciples saw the children coming to be blessed, and they didn't approve. They rebuked the children and their parents. Then Jesus tells His disciples to allow the children to come to Him despite the displeasure it causes them.

As I said above, Longsuffering and Gentleness is how love governs our attitudes towards the lost. **We must exhibit longsuffering toward those that are of a hard heart**. We are longsuffering towards family members that will not hear, and have no interest in the Gospel. We are longsuffering toward the rude and verbally abusive boss. People that are hard (or even impossible) to reach with the love of God, until the stony ground of their heart is plowed and made ready. When we find ourselves in a situation of conflict or opposition with another, we are to have an attitude of longsuffering... allowing them to continue as they are despite the displeasure or pain it causes us, until the time comes when their eyes are opened and their heart is ready to receive the love of God.

We are to suffer them, just as God suffers us.

I charge thee therefore before God, and the Lord Jesus Christ, who shall judge the quick and the dead at his appearing and his kingdom; Preach the word; be instant in

season, out of season; **reprove, rebuke, exhort with all longsuffering and doctrine.**
2 Timothy 4:1-2

That longsuffering attitude is to be supplemented and supported by doctrine. How this doctrine comes into play is governed by other aspects of the fruit. It must be tempered by kindness, and as we will see in a bit, and by meekness. Be forewarned, for we live in a time and age when some will not hear, some will not heed, some will even violently react to the Word of God. If we continue in these verses from 2nd Timothy...

For the time will come when they will not endure sound doctrine; but after their own lusts shall they heap to themselves teachers, having itching ears; And they shall turn away their ears from the truth, and shall be turned unto fables.
2 Timothy 4:3-4

The fruit of Longsuffering is seen in our lives by the way we feel about offenses. Remember, we are still talking about our attitudes... our internal feelings and frame of mind when dealing with people that are hardhearted. Notice that they must endure sound doctrine. Sound doctrine is something that cannot change, therefore it must be endured. Further clarifying the difference between suffering and enduring.

Gentleness is at the other end of the spectrum. **Gentleness is how love governs our attitude towards those that come to us**

brokenhearted and spiritually troubled. When we encounter those that are down-trodden or spiritually broken, **we must handle them with gentleness**... not condemnation, or judgment or indignation... but gentleness.

> We then that are strong ought to **bear the infirmities of the weak**, and not to please ourselves. Let every one of us **please his neighbour for his good to edification**. For even Christ **pleased not himself**; but, as it is written, The reproaches of them that reproached thee fell on me.
> Romans 15:1-3

Notice that the verse just noted from Romans and the earlier verse about longsuffering have something in common. Suffering is allowing despite our displeasure, and we are to bear the infirmities of the weak for their pleasure. What they have in common is that it is not about us and our pleasure. It is about what is pleasing to God. If we are motivated by our own pleasure or edification, then the fruit we are bearing is for us, it is fulfilling our need, and we have our reward. Lets take a look at how this gentleness shows up in the life of Paul ...

> For yourselves, brethren, know our entrance in unto you, that it was not in vain: But even after that we had suffered before, and were shamefully entreated, as ye know, at Philippi, we were bold in our God to speak unto you the gospel of God with much contention. For our exhortation was not of deceit, nor of uncleanness, nor in guile: But

43

as we were allowed of God to be put in trust with the gospel, even so we speak; not as pleasing men, but God, which trieth our hearts. For neither at any time used we flattering words, as ye know, nor a cloke of covetousness; God is witness: Nor of men sought we glory, neither of you, nor yet of others, when we might have been burdensome, as the apostles of Christ. **But we were gentle among you, even as a nurse cherisheth her children: So being affectionately desirous of you, we were willing to have imparted unto you, not the gospel of God only, but also our own souls, because ye were dear unto us.**
1 Thessalonians 2:1-8

These are powerful verses when put into the context of handling the broken in spirit. Even after being shamefully misused and abused by others, they still act as a nursemaid caring for her children... that is how we are to care for those that come to us in need of the love of God. The last thing a genuinely broken person should ever hear from a Christian is "I told you so" or "you should have listened to me" or "what were you thinking" or some other self-righteous nonsense. We might feel justified in doing so, but it is not about our justification or about us being right. It is about hearing and heeding the Spirit of God. Even if that person is coming from a lifestyle that we find reprehensible. That means that yes, even the drug addict, and the thief, and the homosexual, and the drunk, and the porn addict, and the gambler, and the child molester... we are to have gentleness towards them all. If they have come to Christ with a broken spirit and a genuine desire to leave that worldliness behind them, we must receive them with kindness, or we will turn them away from the door of God's house and their blood may be on our hands. It does not mean that we are to blindly trust them and openly accept what they have done or are doing... they still have to endure the consequences of their past actions (as we all do), but our kindness toward them should not be one of those sacrifices. You can kindly disagree, and loving correct and admonish them, condemning the action without condemnation of the person and their spiritual needs.

Pay close attention to this verse from Psalms:

> **The LORD is nigh unto them that are of a broken heart**; and saveth such as be of a contrite spirit.
> Psalms 34:18

I would hate to have a hard heart and speak words of condemnation knowing that the Lord is so close to those that are brokenhearted. It may be that at that moment God is wanting to save that person having the contrite spirit, and you are the instrument which God is wanting to use. But instead of sharing God's love with them, they feel that they are condemned and belittled in the presence of the God that wants to save them. What an awkward and undesirable position to be in.

Take note also that in the verse from Thessalonians, Paul is not using the excuse of being mistreated at the hands of the Philippians as a reason to distance himself from the needs of

Thessaloníki . The sad truth is that bad things happen to good people. We are all too often hurt and misused, sometimes very deeply wounded, but we cannot allow that to become an excuse to be hard and unforgiving to those that need the love of God. These verses from James aptly apply on this topic.

> But the wisdom that is from above is **first pure, then peaceable, gentle, and easy to be intreated, full of mercy and good fruits, without partiality, and without hypocrisy.** And the fruit of righteousness is sown in peace of them that make peace.
> James 3:17-18

Many will use the call to speak the truth as an excuse to be cruel and heartless in what they say and how they say it. Using the explanation of "I was just telling the truth". But wisdom, if it is from above (meaning Godly wisdom), is first pure (undefiled and free of opinion) then it is peaceable and gentle and full of mercy and good fruit. Godly wisdom and Spiritual truth to the broken-spirited is never harsh in its presentation. All of this is further exemplified for us by Christ, our perfect example.

> For when we were yet without strength, in due time **Christ died for the ungodly**. For scarcely for a righteous man will one die: yet peradventure for a good man some would even dare to die. But **God commendeth his love toward us, in that, while we were yet sinners, Christ died for us.**
> Romans 5:6-8

And it came to pass, that, as Jesus sat at meat in his house, **many publicans and sinners sat also together with Jesus** and his disciples: **for there were many, and they followed him.** And when the scribes and Pharisees saw him eat with publicans and sinners, they said unto his disciples, How is it that he eateth and drinketh with publicans and sinners? When Jesus heard it, he saith unto them, They that are whole have no need of the physician, but they that are sick: **I came not to call the righteous, but sinners to repentance.**
Mark 2:15-17

Just as Christ called us out of the muck and mire of our lives unto His righteousness, He is still calling others unto Him. We should be there with a loving gentle hand to help those taking those first steps out of the lives they want to leave behind. His love for sinners, which lead Him to the cross, should dwell in us and shine through our every deed... and there are **MANY** that need that love! Do the loving lights of longsuffering and gentleness shine through you in your dealings with the world? They should. If it were not for that light shining through someone else, YOU would have never known the grace of God. Let it shine and pass on the blessing!

Part 5
The Fruit of Goodness and Faith

We have seen how Joy and Peace is how love governs our attitude towards our circumstances, and how Longsuffering and Gentleness is how love governs our attitude towards the Lost. **Goodness and Faith is how love governs our *actions* towards others.** Up to this point we have been talking about our internal thoughts and feelings. We are venturing into the external now. Our actions. *What we do* not just how we feel about it. Let us take a look at these scriptures about goodness.

> Now the God of hope fill you with all **joy and peace in believing,** that ye may abound in hope, through the **power of the Holy Ghost.** And I myself also am persuaded of you, my brethren, that ye also are **full of goodness, filled with all knowledge, able also to admonish one another.**
> Romans 15:13-14

> Wherefore also we pray always for you, that our God would count you worthy of this calling, and **fulfil all the good pleasure of his goodness**, and the work of faith with power: **That the name of our Lord Jesus Christ may be glorified in you, and ye in him, according to the grace of our God and the Lord Jesus Christ.**
> 2 Thessalonians 1:11-12

> And he said unto him, Why callest thou me good? **there is none good but one, that is, God**: but if thou wilt enter into life, keep the commandments.
> Matthew 19:17

We are told in these verses to be filled with goodness, thereby fulfilling His goodness, but then we are told that there are none good but God. So, how can we *do* that good to *fulfill* His goodness if we cannot *be* good? Sounds like a tongue twister or a riddle. The answer lies in being filled with His Spirit.

We are filled with His Spirit, which **is good**, then our actions motivated by that Spirit are expressions of His goodness **through** us. The Spirit is God in us, who is the **only good** according to Christ. Again, this comes right back to allowing ourselves to live in subjection to God on the throne of our hearts. We will say more about this in a moment. But first we must answer a question.

What is Goodness? What does it look like when it is manifested in our lives, or through us into the lives of others? Matthew tells it like this.

> Give not that which is holy unto the dogs, neither cast ye your pearls before swine, lest they trample them under their feet, and turn again and rend you. Ask, and it shall be given you; seek, and ye shall find; knock, and it shall be opened unto you: For every one that asketh receiveth; and he that seeketh findeth; and to him that knocketh it shall be opened. Or what man is there of you, whom if his son ask bread, will he give him a stone? Or if he ask a fish, will he give him a serpent? **If ye then, being evil, know how to give good gifts unto your children**, how much more shall your Father

which is in heaven give good things to them
that ask him? Therefore all things
whatsoever ye would that men should do to
you, do ye even so to them: for this is the law
and the prophets.
Matthew 7:6-12

These verses show us that goodness is not
dependent upon righteousness, or holiness. So
called "good deeds" can be done by the most vile of
people. Ask anyone on the street if they think they
are a good person... most will answer "yes". But
there is a difference between doing good and being
good. An evil person can *do* good, but only God *is*
good. A person, lost or saved, can do a good deed.
What is in question is the motivation behind the
good deed. This is often a hard question to answer
because the line drawn between intentions and
inclination is often very fuzzy. Is it our own desire
to do good (what we believe to be right), or are we
acting on the goodness of God in us? It's a hard
question. Here are few witnesses of goodness in
scripture to help us make sense of it.

Ye have heard that it hath been said, Thou
shalt love thy neighbour, and hate thine
enemy. But I say unto you, Love your
enemies, bless them that curse you, **do
good to them that hate you,** and pray for
them which despitefully use you, and
persecute you; That ye may be the children
of your Father which is in heaven: for he
maketh his sun to rise on the evil and on the
good, and sendeth rain on the just and on
the unjust. For if ye love them which love
you, what reward have ye? do not even the

publicans the same? And if ye salute your brethren only, what do ye more than others? do not even the publicans so? **Be ye therefore perfect, even as your Father which is in heaven is perfect.**
Matthew 5:43-48

And another example:

But I say unto you which hear, **Love your enemies, do good to them which hate you, Bless them that curse you, and pray for them which despitefully use you. And unto him that smiteth thee on the one cheek offer also the other; and him that taketh away thy cloke forbid not to take thy coat also.** Give to every man that asketh of thee; and of him that taketh away thy goods ask them not again. **And as ye would that men should do to you, do ye also to them likewise.** For if ye love them which love you, what thank have ye? for sinners also love those that love them. **And if ye do good to them which do good to you, what thank have ye? for sinners also do even the same.** And if ye lend to them of whom ye hope to receive, what thank have ye? for sinners also lend to sinners, to receive as much again. **But love ye your enemies, and do good, and lend, hoping for nothing again; and your reward shall be great, and ye shall be the children of the Highest: <u>for he is kind unto the unthankful and to the evil.</u>**
Luke 6:27-35

Living out this goodness as we are asked can be difficult and sometimes impossible. The line of God's goodness and our own idea of right and wrong is drawn here in the treatment of our enemies. How do we treat our enemies? It is easy to do good to someone you love and care for. It is a different story to do Godly goodness to someone you despise. This ties right back into what we are talking about with gentleness. Do we act in all situations with God's goodness in our hearts? We can do a good thing but with a spiteful spirit. We must ensure that our motivations are pure. That can be accomplished with this one simple test question. Why am I doing it? If it is to "heap coals on their heads", then you are wrong. You are doing it out of spite. Is it "because it's the right thing to do?" If so, by who's standard? God's or yours, or your parent's, or your pastor's? This is often a hard question to answer. My estimation at this time is it's best when you can't tell the difference between your motivations and God's motivating Spirit. (When we are so in tune with God's will that we can't see a discernible difference between our thoughts and His.) This requires absolute honesty with yourself and your own internal dialogue. We will talk more about that in the section on Honesty.

We must also ask, do these verses from above tell us that we are to voluntarily suffer the abuse of others without end? Does this mean for us to become the punching bag or object of ridicule without taking any action? Not at all! Just a few verses before that, we have a phrase that gives us a more complete picture of this.

Blessed are ye, **when men shall hate you, and when they shall separate you from their company**, and shall reproach you, and cast out your name as evil, for the Son of man's sake.
Luke 6:22

Abusive people will voluntarily remove themselves from us, because the goodness of God coming through us will be reprehensible to them. And if they speak evil of you... so what! I can assure you that you are not the only person they have mistreated, and others will know the truth of your character better by their disparaging words. Not only will they separate themselves from us because of their searing conscience, but we are not asked to just stand there and take it. A one-time chance encounter is what these verses are talking about. Not a long term passive acceptance of abuse. Take these other verses into consideration.

Now I beseech you, brethren, **mark them which cause divisions and offences contrary to the doctrine** which ye have learned; **and avoid them.**
Romans 16:17

O Timothy, keep that which is committed to thy trust, **avoiding profane and vain babblings, and oppositions of science falsely so called**: Which some professing have erred concerning the faith. Grace be with thee. Amen.
1 Timothy 6:20-21

But **foolish and unlearned questions**

avoid, knowing that they do gender strifes.
2 Timothy 2:23

But **avoid** foolish questions, and genealogies, and contentions, and strivings about the law; for they are unprofitable and vain. A man that is an heretick **after the first and second admonition reject;** Knowing that he that is such is subverted, and sinneth, being condemned of himself.
Titus 3:9-11

If a person has a tendency to create contention or strife in your life, avoid that person. If a person is abusive or untrustworthy, avoid them. If the person is of enough importance to you that you feel a need to confront them for their actions, and they do not acknowledge their wrong doing and attempt to change, reject them. We do not have to stand in silent acceptance of wrongdoing, whether it be at the hands of a stranger or a family member or even a spouse. We will learn more about this concept when we take a look at Biblical meekness.

I use this example when trying to illustrate these concepts. If a person has been invited to your home, and they steal something from your bedroom, and you know it, avoid having them in your house ever again. There is no sin in that. People (usually unsaved people who know a little scripture) are always throwing "judge not lest ye be judged" back at Christians who stand their ground in matters like this. But when we look at the full meaning of that scripture instead of taking a few words out of context, we see something different.

Be ye therefore merciful, as your Father also is merciful. **Judge not, and ye shall not be judged:** condemn not, and ye shall not be condemned: forgive, and ye shall be forgiven: Give, and it shall be given unto you; good measure, pressed down, and shaken together, and running over, shall men give into your bosom. **For with the same measure that ye mete withal it shall be measured to you again.**
Luke 6:36-38

What the scripture is saying in its fullness is what ever standard you use to judge another, you will be judged by. If you are doing your best to live by the standards set forth in God's Word as you understand it, and you are judging by those standards, you are doing exactly what the the Bible is asking you to do. This judgment must be tempered by the other fruit we have discussed when dealing with others... we must do all things with love, and maintain an attitude of longsuffering and gentleness for others in our hearts.

Therefore thou art **inexcusable, O man**, whosoever thou art that judgest: for **wherein thou judgest another, thou condemnest thyself; for thou that judgest doest the same things.** But we are sure that **the judgment of God is according to truth against them which commit such things.** And thinkest thou this, **O man, that judgest them which do such things, and doest the same, that thou shalt escape the judgment of God?**
Romans 2:1-3

These verses (again popular for condemnation of judgment) are directed at those that call out the sin of another but persist in their own similar sin. Paul is calling out those that draw attention to the wrong doing of others to make themselves appear more righteous.

Goodness, therefore, is expressed in treating those who use and abuse us, ridicule and even hate us simply because we call ourselves Christian, with love and kindness. But it is **NOT** allowing ourselves to be a continual target of this abuse. We have, with the strength of the Spirit, the ability and permission to avoid or even reject those that are constantly contentious or abusive towards us.

> For this cause I bow my knees unto the Father of our Lord Jesus Christ, Of whom the whole family in heaven and earth is named, That he would grant you, according to the riches of his glory, **to be strengthened with might by his Spirit in the inner man**; **That Christ may dwell in your hearts by faith**; that ye, being rooted and grounded in **love**, May be able to comprehend with all saints what is the breadth, and length, and depth, and height; And to know the love of Christ, which passeth knowledge, **that ye might be filled with all the fulness of God.**
> Ephesians 3:14-19

Again we have the fullness of God in us through goodness. In fact the whole Godhead is on board this time. The *Spirit* is strengthening the inner man to have the faith that *Christ* might dwell in us and allow us to be filled with fullness of *God*.

So, with this understanding of goodness... seeing that none are truly good without the indwelling Spirit of God, and it is not the person that is good (righteous or wicked) it is the action that is deemed good... then only those actions that are motivated by the love of God in us can truly be good. We are therefore to treat every person with goodness. We are to endeavor to make every action of our lives motivated by the love of God in us. Can we do this in everything? Can every action be inspired by loving thoughts toward and from God? Absolutely! At the home, every choice and action can give honour to God. At work, every task can be done as unto the Lord. When interacting with others we can (and should) treat them with love and respect... even if we are in disagreement with them. That is how love is fulfilled through goodness in our actions towards others.

Now lets learn something about faith...

Faith

Now faith is the substance of things hoped for, the evidence of things not seen.
Hebrews 11:1

We often use this verse to give an answer for the faith that we have and why we believe in that which cannot be seen. **Faith** is the foundation of Christianity, and the beginning of our spiritual rebirth. It is through faith in Christ that we first come to truly know God. It is through faith in His promises that we are able to be longsuffering and endure those things in which we see no blessing. Faith in who He is and what He is able to do.

> But **without faith *it is* impossible to please *him*: for he that cometh to God must believe that he is**, and *that* **he is a rewarder** of them that diligently seek him.
> Hebrews 11:6

It is not just a belief in God and His Son. As we pointed out in the Introduction, even the devils believe and tremble at His name. It is faith in the fact that He IS God, and IS able to do that which HE says He will do. We must ask ourselves if we truly believe that God **IS!** Not just some metaphysical manifestation, or some ideological vision of goodness... but that **He IS**. He exists, is real, is effectual in our lives, is all knowing and all powerful and creator of all... AND that He IS the rewarder of those that seek Him. This reward implies two things: first, that there is a decision made as to who gets rewarded. (Or in simpler terms, that there is a judgment.) Second, that it is incumbent on our part to seek Him to be rewarded. This is going to step on some toes, but those that say they are Christian and do not believe in judgment (reward for the faithful seekers and punishment for the faithless) are betraying their so called faith. If they are betraying this faith by denying that He is the rewarder of those that seek him, then (as the verse tells us) they cannot please Him. Faith is so much more than just the substance of things hoped for and evidence of things unseen. It is the means by which we are able to enter into the relationship with our God and the only means by which we can please Him.

We have seen that **Goodness is how Love governs our actions towards others in our daily interactions. Faith is the counterpart to that and is how love governs our actions in response to God.**

We have shown how important faith is in establishing our relationship with God.

> For by **grace are ye saved through faith**; and that not of yourselves: it is the gift of God: **Not of works, lest any man should boast**.
> Ephesians 2:8-9

It is by grace (undeserved favor) that we are saved, but we must have faith to receive that grace.

Faith in what?

We have already pointed out that we must have faith that God is, and that He is the rewarder (or judge). But there are other things that we **must** have faith in as well.

> For if the dead rise not, then is not Christ raised: And **if Christ be not raised, your faith is vain; ye are yet in your sins.** Then they also which are fallen asleep in Christ are perished.
> 1 Corinthians 15:16-18

We must also have faith in the fact that Christ has risen from the dead. If He did not conquer the grave, then we are still dead in our sins.

> Whom **God hath set forth to be a propitiation <u>through faith in his blood</u>**, to declare his righteousness for the remission of sins that are past, through the forbearance of God;
> Romans 3:25

We must also have faith in the blood that was shed for us. His resurrection gives life, but His blood gives us the remission of sins.

> Beloved, believe not every spirit, but try the spirits whether they are of God: because many false prophets are gone out into the world. Hereby know ye the Spirit of God: **Every spirit that confesseth that Jesus Christ is come in the flesh is of God: And every spirit that confesseth not that Jesus Christ is come in the flesh is not of God: and this is that spirit of**

antichrist, whereof ye have heard that it should come; and even now already is it in the world.
1 John 4:1-3

We must also believe that Christ was sent by God and...

And **without controversy** great is the mystery of godliness: **God was manifest in the flesh**, justified in the Spirit, seen of angels, preached unto the Gentiles, believed on in the world, **received up into glory**.
1 Timothy 3:16

...God was manifest in the flesh in the person of Jesus Christ. This is something that we **must** have faith in.

In a nut shell, the Bible tells us that we must have faith in the fact that God is, and He is the judge of mankind. We must have faith in the resurrection of Jesus. We must have faith in the sin atoning blood of Christ. We must have faith in the fact that God is manifest in the flesh in the person of Jesus Christ.

If we do not have faith in these core concepts, then we are not of God, but are an antichrist, (1 John 4) and we cannot please God (Hebrews 11:6). This is what we must have to call ourselves a child of God. Now lets take a look at how this faith applies to our daily lives in helping us to discern the Spirit of God.

As we have already seen, goodness is how love governs our *actions* towards those that are in the world. We are to treat every individual with goodness. **Faith, however, is how love governs our *actions* towards God.** Not only our initial faith at the time of salvation, or our diligence in reading the Bible or going to Church. It is a trust in Christ, and that He has and will continue to fulfill the promises that He has made to us.

> But unto every one of us is given grace according to **the measure of the gift of Christ.**
> Ephesians 4:7

> For I say, through the grace given unto me, to every man that is among you, not to think of himself more highly than he ought to think; but to think soberly, according as **God hath dealt to <u>every man</u> the measure of faith**.
> Romans 12:3

Take note of the phrasing concerning "the" measure of faith. This is a simple distinction but is so profound in its application. I know that all of us of faith, at one time or another, have said or thought "I wish I had faith like that"... or "I don't know if I have the faith to do..." whatever. When we look on another and see the faith they are exercising in their lives we need to recall this phrase, "the measure of faith".

God in His wisdom has given every one "the" measure of faith. It is not *a* measure, but *the* measure. This speaks of a specific amount. A measure, for example, could be a half cup, or a quarter cup or a full cup... it is a measure. But the measure is a specific one. It may be the one I am pointing at as I speak, or (as in this case) the only measure. The only size it comes in. We can see this evidenced in other places in scripture.

> Then Peter opened his mouth, and said, Of a truth **I perceive that God is no respecter of persons**: But in every nation he that feareth him, and worketh righteousness, is accepted with him.
> Acts 10:34-35

> For there is **no respect of persons with God**.
> Romans 2:11

> And, ye masters, do the same things unto them, forbearing threatening: knowing that your Master also is in heaven; **neither is there respect of persons with him**.
> Ephesians 6:9

God is not a respecter of persons. He does not deal out His gift of faith greater to this one and less to that one. He does not care if you are rich or poor, man or woman, tall or short, black or white. He gives to every man the measure of faith. The question we must ask is not how much faith do we have, but how much other stuff is there over-shadowing the measure of faith we have been given? How many other things have your attention and your time? What other things occupy your thoughts and fill your days? God has given to you, dear reader, the same amount of faith that He gave to Peter and Paul and Stephen. The trouble we have these days is that the ratio of faith to worldly interests is out of balance. The amount of faith does not change. Yes, I said the amount of faith does not change. What changes is the amount of worldly influences in our lives in comparison to that measure of faith.

> And the apostles said unto the Lord, **Increase our faith**. And the Lord said, If ye had faith as a grain of mustard seed, ye might say unto this sycamine tree, Be thou plucked up by the root, and be thou planted in the sea; and it should obey you. **But** which of you, having a servant plowing or feeding cattle, will say unto him by and by, when he is come from the field, Go and sit down to meat? And will not rather say unto him, Make ready wherewith I may sup, and gird thyself, and serve me, till I have eaten and drunken; **and afterward thou shalt eat and drink?** Doth he thank that servant because he did the things that were commanded him? I trow not. **So likewise ye, when ye shall have done all those things which are commanded you, say, We are unprofitable servants: we have done that which was our duty to do.**
> Luke 17:5-10

When we look at these verses where the apostles are asking the Lord to increase their faith, He tells them of the mustard seed... BUT that time will not be fulfilled until our works or our duties are completed, and the serving of the master is fulfilled. Then we will see the growth of faith.

When we look at the answer in its fullness, we see that the growth of the faith is contingent upon us fulfilling the task assigned to us by the master of the house. That task has not yet been fulfilled. What we have now is the earnest of the Spirit. We have the measure given to all, but the fullness will not be realized until the master is satisfied. Then and only then can we sit at the Master's table and be fed. The complete task of Christ and His Church are not yet realized. He came once as a lamb to the slaughter, but He will return again as a King and Lord to rule and reign.

> For David is not ascended into the heavens: but he saith himself, The LORD said unto my Lord, Sit thou on my right hand, **Until I make thy foes thy footstool.** Therefore let all the house of Israel know assuredly, that God hath made that same Jesus, whom ye have crucified, both Lord and Christ.
> Acts 2:34-36

> But this man, after he had offered one sacrifice for sins for ever, sat down on the right hand of God; From henceforth expecting **till his enemies be made his footstool.**
> Hebrews 10:12-13

> For it is written, **As I live, saith the Lord, every knee shall bow to me, and every tongue shall confess to God.**
> Romans 14:11

> That **at the name of Jesus every knee should bow**, of things in heaven, and

things in earth, and things under the earth;
Philippians 2:10

The master's task will not be complete until all the world is under His rule. Then the fullness of our faith will be realized. The work that was finished on the Cross was the redemptive work of mankind, it was not the establishment of Christ as king.

The measure of faith we are given here is the same for all, for He is not a respecter of persons. Instead, it is how much other stuff we pile on top of our faith that determines how that faith shines through us. So when we see another that seems to have so much more faith than ourselves, what we really need to ask is "Why isn't my faith shining like theirs?" "What is overshadowing or drowning out the faith I have?" That is the real question. This fruit of faith is manifest in our daily walk in the unquestioning and unrelenting belief that God IS and is the rewarder of those that seek Him. We will not always get it right. We will have doubts about His purpose and plan for us, but if we diligently seek Him, we will not lose sight of Him. Seek Him daily!

In summary, when we are faced with a circumstance where we are not sure of how to approach a person, we must focus our attention on what is good. And good does not always mean that it is what will appease the person or make them happy. An extreme example would be giving money to a drug addict. It would make him feel better to have the money to temporarily satisfy his needs, but it is not good for him. What would be good is getting him some help, or better yet, helping him find the Lord. We can know what is good in any situation by asking ourselves this simple question. "What would be pleasing to God?" Remember that He is the only true good and the source of all that is good in us.

Just as we should aim to please God in our dealings with others, we should also aim to be pleasing to God in our actions towards Him. Do we take His word seriously? Do we do, in faith, those things He has asked us to do, not concerning ourselves with the opinions of others? Do we refrain from doing those things He has told us not to do? In short, do you believe God is who He says He is? This could be the most the important question you will ever ask yourself.

Part 6
The Fruit of Meekness and Temperance

We have seen how Joy and Peace are how love governs our attitudes towards our circumstances, how Longsuffering governs our attitude towards the hardhearted, Gentleness governs our attitude toward the brokenhearted and spiritually troubled. Goodness is what governs our actions towards all, and Faith is what governs our actions towards God.

Meekness and Temperance is how love governs those in opposition to God. **Meekness specifically, is how love governs our response to the people of God, that are in opposition to God.**

> Seek ye the LORD, all ye meek of the earth, which have wrought his judgment; **seek righteousness, seek meekness: it may be ye shall be hid in <u>the day of the LORD'S anger.</u>**
> Zephaniah 2:3

> Now I Paul myself beseech you by the **meekness and gentleness** of Christ, who in presence am base among you, but being absent am bold toward you:
> 2 Corinthians 10:1

> **Blessed are the meek: <u>for they shall inherit the earth.</u>**
> Matthew 5:5

When we read these verses, we see there is a strong connection between meekness and the end times. There are literally dozens of times that being meek is directly associated with the day of the Lord and end times events and judgment.

71

I am about to shatter our traditional understanding of meekness. For generations we have had a non-Biblical understanding of meekness. For us to understand what meekness is, we must look at Moses.

Why Moses?

> (Now the man Moses was very meek, above all the men which were upon the face of the earth.)
> Numbers 12:3

The Bible tells us very simply and clearly that Moses was the most meek man upon the earth. So, next to Christ, Moses is our best example of meekness. We have this idea that meekness is turning the other cheek, being of a mild character, being soft spoken and non-confrontational. Not so! Let us take a look at a few Biblical example of Moses meekness.

> With him will I speak mouth to mouth, even apparently, and not in dark speeches; and the similitude of the LORD shall he behold: wherefore then were ye not afraid to speak against my servant Moses?
> Numbers 12:8

In these verse from Numbers 12, Aaron and Miriam have just challenged Moses for taking an Ethiopian wife. The response of God is seen in striking Miriam with leprosy. Moses reacted in meekness.

> And Moses cried unto the LORD, saying,

Heal her now, O God, I beseech thee.
Numbers 12:13

Another example to help illustrate the whole picture:

> They have turned aside quickly out of the way which I commanded them: they have made them a molten calf, and have worshipped it, and have sacrificed thereunto, and said, These be thy gods, O Israel, which have brought thee up out of the land of Egypt. **And the LORD said unto Moses, I have seen this people, and, behold, it is a stiffnecked people: Now therefore let me alone, that my wrath may wax hot against them, and that I may consume them: and I will make of thee a great nation.** And **Moses besought the LORD his God, and said, LORD, why doth thy wrath wax hot against thy people, which thou hast brought forth out of the land of Egypt with great power, and with a mighty hand?** Wherefore should the Egyptians speak, and say, For mischief did he bring them out, to slay them in the mountains, and to consume them from the face of the earth? Turn from thy fierce wrath, and repent of this evil against thy people. Remember Abraham, Isaac, and Israel, thy servants, to whom thou swarest by thine own self, and saidst unto them, I will multiply your seed as the stars of heaven, and all this land that I have spoken of will I give unto your seed, and they shall inherit it for ever. **And the**

LORD repented of the evil which he thought to do unto his people.
Exodus 32:8-14

In both of these examples, Moses responded to the judgment of God with a prayer of intercession to God on behalf of the people. Notice though, that these are people that called themselves the people of God, but they had quickly gotten out of the will of God; challenging the authority of Moses and worshiping the golden calf. But we are not done. Lets take a look at how Moses responded to these people.

> Then Moses stood in the gate of the camp, and said, **Who is on the LORD'S side? let him come unto me**. And all the sons of Levi gathered themselves together unto him. And he said unto them, Thus saith the LORD God of Israel, **Put every man his sword by his side, and go in and out from gate to gate throughout the camp, and slay every man his brother, and every man his companion, and every man his neighbour.** And the children of Levi did according to the word of Moses: and there fell of the people that day about three thousand men.
> Exodus 32:26-28

Moses was not a mild mannered man. He is referred to as the most meek, but he was not passive when it came to the Word of God. He was passionate about making sure the will of God was known and enforced among the people of God. But that passion about God's instructions was partnered with earnest and heartfelt intercession for God's people.

We can see the same pattern of behavior in the situation in Numbers 16. In this event Korah challenged the authority of Moses as being the prophet of God. God's response is very clear.

> Separate yourselves from among this congregation, that I may consume them in a moment.
> Numbers 16:21

God's response is of destruction and judgment. But Moses immediately responded:

> And they (Moses and Aaron) fell upon their faces, and said, **O God, the God of the spirits of all flesh, shall one man sin, and wilt thou be wroth with all the congregation?** (parentheses added)
> Numbers 16:22

Meekness is not passivity or a quiet demeanor. Meekness is a *passion* for the Word of the Lord, and a *compassion* for the people of God which are out of God's will. This passion is indicated in Moses' first few words to Pharaoh.

> And afterward Moses and Aaron went in, and told Pharaoh, **Thus saith the LORD God of Israel**, Let my people go, that they may hold a feast unto me in the wilderness.
> Exodus 5:1

"Thus saith the Lord." Meekness is a reverence and passionate response for the Word of the Lord.

Another thing that these examples have in common is that Moses interceded before God for the people of God... even when they were offensive to him. This being the case, then Christ is by far the most meek that has ever lived. Not because He was passive, He wasn't. He cleansed God's house twice, and called the Pharisees vipers and hypocrites and sepulchers full of dead men's bones to their faces. He was not a pacifist. In fact, He is just the opposite.

> **Suppose ye that I am come to give peace on earth? I tell you, Nay; but rather division**: For from henceforth there shall be five in one house divided, three against two, and two against three. The father shall be divided against the son, and the son against the father; the mother against the daughter, and the daughter against the mother; the mother in law against her daughter in law, and the daughter in law against her mother in law. Luke 12:51-53

He did not bring peace... but a peace of mind to those that believe on Him. He had (and inspired) a passionate boldness for the Word of God, and a compassion for God's elect causing Him to want to intercede for them before an awesome God. He is still making intercession for us today while He sits on the right hand of God, and He will return some day, not with an olive branch of peace in His hand, but a sharp two-edged sword coming out of His mouth, with which He will slay His enemies. Amen! How passive and mild mannered is that?

Peter exhibited this same kind of meekness on the day of Pentecost.

But Peter, standing up with the eleven, lifted up his voice, and said unto them, Ye men of Judaea, and all ye that dwell at Jerusalem, be this known unto you, and hearken to my words:
Acts 2:14

This is a different idea of meekness... but much more Biblical than what we are used to hearing. When we look at Christ, Moses, Peter, Stephen and even Paul as our examples we see that we are to be passionate about ensuring that the Word of God is known and applied, but also intercede for those that have strayed from the truth by calling out on their behalf before an awesome God. *That* is Biblical Meekness.

Now that we can see that meekness is how love governs our actions towards those in opposition to God, **Temperance is how love governs our actions toward ourselves, our own flesh, which is in opposition to God.**

And as he reasoned of righteousness, **temperance,** and judgment to come, Felix trembled, and answered, Go thy way for this time; when I have a convenient season, I will call for thee.
Acts 24:25

And to knowledge **temperance**; and to temperance patience; and to patience godliness;
2 Peter 1:6

Next to the listing of the fruit of the Spirit in Galatians, these are the only times that temperance appears in the entire Bible. Its dictionary definition is having the quality of or being temperant. Which means masterful. These following verses are the most telling of temperance. We tend to think of it as self control, but it is more than self control... it is *mastery* over the self and the flesh.

> **And every man that striveth for the mastery is temperate in all things.** Now they do it to obtain a corruptible crown; but we an incorruptible.
> 1 Corinthians 9:25

> Dearly beloved, I beseech you as strangers and pilgrims, **abstain from fleshly lusts, which war against the soul**; Having your conversation honest among the Gentiles: **that, whereas they speak against you as evildoers, they may by your good works, which they shall behold, glorify God** in the day of visitation.
> 1 Peter 2:11-12

Abstain, refrain from, the satisfying of the flesh so that your good works shall glorify God. All too often we find our culture in an atmosphere of "do as I say, not as I do", when it is so much more true that "I cannot hear what you are saying because I see what you do." When we are constantly giving in to the flesh we are short-circuiting and circumventing the good works we may be doing.

The fruit of temperance, my friends, is by far the most difficult aspect of the fruit of the Spirit to stay true to. In the introduction we talked about Spiritual warfare and how there is a constant struggle between that which is of God and that which is not. We saw how we could avoid or even reject those that are constantly contentious or offensive. We can walk away from contentious people or tempting situations, but we cannot avoid ourselves. We cannot walk away from the driving forces of our flesh and worldly hearts. We cannot rid ourselves of these inclinations, but we can gain temperance. We can, through Christ, have mastery over them. We need to understand that mastery is different than control. Look at it like this, you can control a dog by putting it on a leash. It may bark and snarl all day long, but it is under control in that it cannot do any harm. But mastery is the snapping of the fingers or the sound of your voice that hushes the dog. Temperance is not controlling the flesh, as in keeping it from running out of control, but a training of the flesh to have mastery over it and keeping it in submission to the spirit. We will learn more about this in the next section on Spiritual Warfare.

So, when you look at where you stand for God, do you find yourself satisfying the Biblical definition of meekness? Are you firm in your understanding of God's Word... firm enough to defend it? Firm enough to be bold about it? And do you find your prayer life at least speckled with intercession for those that you know and care for that are falling away from the strait and narrow path? This is where we all should be. Passionate about God's Word, and compassionate towards God's people.

Next we must ask ourselves... and this is a hard one... who is in charge of you? Who has the mastery? Does your spirit serve your flesh, or is your flesh in subjection to the Spirit? If we are honest with ourselves, we would have a hard time answering this one. Let me put it into more practical terms. How hard was it to resist eating that snack the other day that you knew you should not have? Did you take an extra hard look at the lady in the mini-shirt? Did you buy that new tool, knowing that you really needed that money to fix the washing machine? Where did your eyes wander on the internet last night? Do you still smoke... drink... overeat? (Ouch!) So I will ask again... Who has the mastery?

Part 7
Spiritual Warfare

When we think of Spiritual Warfare, we often have this image in our mind of dark and sinister creatures battling against the angels in heaven and striving over the souls of men. There may be some truth to this, but our part... the area where we must earnestly contend... is in our own hearts. We are, by the very virtue of being a child of God, combatants in a conflict over control of our lives and thoughts. There are two fronts in this fight. The first is hindering the lost from coming into that relationship with God, the second is hindering the child of God from living in God's will. Once a person is saved, the soul is no longer the point of contention. It (the soul) is forever bound to our Lord and Savior. On this front, the conflict is over living in God's will or living in the will of the flesh. Lets take a few moments and look at what it means to be in this battle.

> Thou therefore endure hardness, as a good soldier of Jesus Christ. No man that warreth entangleth himself with the affairs of this life; that he may please him who hath chosen him to be a soldier. And if a man also strive for masteries, yet is he not crowned, except he strive lawfully.
> 2 Timothy 2:3-5

Lets break this down line by line.

> Thou therefore endure hardness, as a good soldier of Jesus Christ.
> 2 Timothy 2:3

A few things are stated here. First, is that there is a trouble or hardness that must be endured. If you recall from our look at the difference between suffering and enduring... this hardness is something that we cannot change. We must endure what we cannot change. Also, by being called a soldier, it implies there is a battle. As a soldier, we are not passive bystanders. We are active combatants in our own daily hardness. Who are we fighting for? Jesus Christ! Not that He needs us to defend Him, but we are fighting for His cause, and for His glory in our own private internal struggle for mastery over our lives and service to Him. Christ tells us, when talking with Paul, that He gets glory out of our infirmities. If there was no battle (the front lines of personal weaknesses), there would be no victory for Christ to claim in our lives. That is why Paul gloried in his infirmities. It is through Christ that we have the ability to have mastery over our infirmities, and therefore through the infirmities that Christ is made victorious.

> No man that warreth entangleth himself with the affairs of this life; that he may please him who hath chosen him to be a soldier.
> 2 Timothy 2:4

No man that is in battle concerns himself with the worries of life. Notice also the use of the word entangle. When in a spiritual fight, thoughts of the affairs of this world are a trap. Christ told us to take no thought of what you might eat or drink or for raiment. Don't worry about tomorrow.

> Take therefore no thought for the morrow: for the morrow shall take thought for the

things of itself. Sufficient unto the day is the evil thereof.
Matthew 6:34

But right before this verse, He commands us to seek first the Kingdom of God. Be in that battle and focus on the conflict at hand. The goal is to bring glory and honor to God and His Son. But all too often thoughts of this world will bog us down. Concerns about time, money, appearances, peer pressure, popularity and on and on. A man preparing to go into conflict is not thinking about how much money he has in the bank or what the neighbors might think or what he is going to eat tomorrow. He may not have a tomorrow. He is focused on how to defeat the enemy at hand. (Finishing out 2 Timothy 2:4) And why do we focus on what is at hand and not the affairs of the world? To please Christ, the one who chose us as a soldier. That is exactly what Paul was talking about when he gloried in his weaknesses.

And if a man also strive for masteries, yet is he not crowned, except he strive lawfully.
2 Timothy 2:5

When a man strives for this mastery over the flesh, he is not crowned if he cheats. If the conflict is within us, then who are we cheating? No one but ourselves. We can, given enough motivation, convince ourselves that we have won a victory over something, when in fact we have just chained up our dog for a bit. He might be chained and muzzled and not be able to make a noise or do any harm, but once loosed (and it will happen), that dog is meaner and harder to control than before. That is cheating in spiritual warfare. That is control over the flesh, not mastery. In the end, the individual is the only one loosing.

Another way that we cheat at this spiritual warfare is by addressing a small issue or a symptom, and avoiding or dismissing the real problem. Examples would be doing away with pornography, but not dealing with the true issue of adultery of the heart or covetousness... resolving a debt, but not addressing the emptiness you try and fill with shopping... not hitting your spouse any more, but not seeking to soften your calloused heart. Its like fighting with a child. The child (or smaller issue) is the offspring (or product) of the parent (real problem). The child is easily knocked down and made to cry. Step up and have an adult fight, and leave the kids alone. They will leave on their own once the parents are out of the picture.

A third way we cheat in spiritual warfare is by deflection. We do this either by pointing out or embellishing the wrong doing of others (therefore drawing attention away from ourselves) or convincing ourselves that "at least I'm not as bad as that guy". There is no glory in these hollow victories.

We discussed earlier in Part 5 on Goodness that there is the measure of faith that is received by every believer. God is no respecter of persons, and whether we are rich or poor, man or woman, tall or short, God is going to place in us the same measure of faith that He gives to all who believe. The key to overcoming the flesh (and having temperance or mastery over it) is in the ration of spirituality to worldliness. Just for clarification, lets look at these verses again.

> But unto every one of us is given grace according to **the measure of the gift of Christ.**
> **Ephesians 4:7**
>
> For I say, through the grace given unto me, to every man that is among you, not to think of himself more highly than he ought to think; but to think soberly, according as **God hath dealt to every man the measure of faith**.
> Romans 12:3

We are given the measure of faith. This earnest of the Spirit, or this portion we receive seals us in God's family until the day we are fully redeemed. How does this measure of faith play into our spiritual conflict? If we are all given the same amount of faith, then the ability of the spirit to prevail in this conflict is determined by the strength we allow the flesh. We cannot increase *the measure* of faith, but we can increase the influence of that faith by decreasing the influence of the world.

There was a time when Jesus had given His disciples the power to cast out all devils.

> Then he called his twelve disciples together, and **gave them power and authority over all devils**, and to cure diseases. And he sent them to preach the kingdom of God, and to heal the sick.
> Luke 9:1-2

The disciples were given power and authority over all devils. But we see just a few verses later, just after Jesus is transfigured, that they are powerless over a devil.

> And, behold, a man of the company cried out, saying, Master, I beseech thee, look upon my son: for he is mine only child. And, lo, a spirit taketh him, and he suddenly crieth out; and it teareth him that he foameth again, and bruising him hardly departeth from him. And **I besought thy disciples to cast him out; and they could not.**
> Luke 9:38-40

We can see in the next verse that Jesus rebukes His disciples for their lack of faith, and casts the devil out Himself.

> And Jesus answering said, O faithless and perverse generation, how long shall I be with you, and suffer you? Bring thy son hither. And as he was yet a coming, the devil threw him down, and tare him. And Jesus rebuked the unclean spirit, and healed the child, and delivered him again to his father.
> Luke 9:41-42

But that is only part of the story. When we look at what the other Gospels have to say about it, Jesus had more to say about the situation than just rebuking His disciples.

> But Jesus took him by the hand, and lifted

him up; and he arose. And when he was come into the house, his disciples asked him privately, Why could not we cast him out? And he said unto them, This kind can come forth by nothing, but by prayer and fasting.
Mark 9:27-29

The disciples asked Him privately why they could not do it. They heard Him say that they lacked faith, but they did not lack faith. He gave them authority over all devils, but Jesus tells them that this *kind* comes out by prayer and fasting only. It is a kind of devil or enemy or affliction that came out by prayer and fasting only. Why fasting?

And **every man that striveth for the mastery is temperate in all things**. Now they do it to obtain a corruptible crown; but we an incorruptible. I therefore so run, not as uncertainly; so fight I, not as one that beateth the air: But **I keep under my body, and bring it into subjection:** lest that by any means, when I have preached to others, I myself should be a castaway.
1 Corinthians 9:25-27

When we talk of fasting, we talk of bringing the flesh into subjection. In the verses above, Paul is keeping his body under control, and bringing it into subjection by moderation in all things. When we fast from food, we do it to focus our attention on the spiritual. But when we fast from the flesh, we stop feeding those things that are fleshly.

For they that are after the flesh do mind the things of the flesh; but they that are after the

Spirit the things of the Spirit. **For to be carnally minded is death**; but to be spiritually minded is life and peace. **Because the carnal mind is enmity against God:** for it is not subject to the law of God, neither indeed can be. So then **they that are in the flesh cannot please God.**
Romans 8:5-8

Fasting is not limited to the food we put in our mouths. We can fast from anything. An alcoholic must fast from alcohol. A person with lust issues must fast from things that encourage or feed that lust. We must, in this spiritual fight, weaken the enemy where the enemy is strongest in our lives, by starving it in those areas. When Christ indicated that there was a kind of enemy that can be defeated only by prayer and fasting, He was not talking about the prayer and fasting of the disciples. If that were the case, Jesus would have continued in His rebuking them for their unbelief. It was not the disciples unbelief. It was the need to pray and fast on the part of the one being oppressed. I can pray for you all day long, but that is not going to make your faith greater. You must pray. I can fast all day long, but that is not going to bring your flesh into subjection. **You** must fast in that area where your flesh is strong, thereby allowing the spirit to prevail over it. We all have an area (or areas) where our flesh is strong and has a greater influence over us. We need to weaken them and not give them room to grow. Paul puts it like this...

But put ye on the Lord Jesus Christ, and make not provision for the flesh, to fulfil the

lusts thereof.
Romans 13:14

Don't even give it a space to operate. Once it has decreased, that space must be filled with edifying and encouraging things.

> Finally, brethren, whatsoever things are true, whatsoever things are honest, whatsoever things are just, whatsoever things are pure, whatsoever things are lovely, whatsoever things are of good report; if there be any virtue, and if there be any praise, think on these things.
> Philippians 4:8

Once the flesh has started to recede, the void must be filled. The Bible instructs us to fill the void with these kinds of things. Or else, the void will be filled by something much less desirable.

> When the unclean spirit is gone out of a man, he walketh through dry places, seeking rest, and findeth none. Then he saith, I will return into my house from whence I came out; and when he is come, he findeth it empty, swept, and garnished. Then goeth he, and taketh with himself seven other spirits more wicked than himself, and they enter in and dwell there: and the last state of that man is worse than the first. Even so shall it be also unto this wicked generation.
> Matthew 12:43-45

Once the wickedness has left the house (which is the man), when it returns to find the house (the man) empty, it will set up house again. The man's heart may be clean, it may be empty of fleshly desires, but if it is not occupied with something else, the behavior will return and reside there again. Only it will not be alone. It will bring friends and the last state of the man is worse than when he started.

So, we must starve the flesh and fill our hearts with edifying things (prayer, scripture reading, Christian fellowship, works, witnessing... etc.) to fill the space that is left behind. In my estimation, that is the essence of internal Spiritual Warfare... edifying that which is Spiritual and starving that which is worldly.

Part 8
Additional Insights

**God will not prompt us to do something
which is in conflict or contradiction to His
already written word. He will not confuse
us.**

> But the LORD is with me as a mighty terrible
> one: therefore my persecutors shall stumble,
> and they shall not prevail: they shall be
> greatly ashamed; for they shall not prosper:
> **their everlasting confusion shall never
> be forgotten.**
> Jeremiah 20:11

The enemies of God are the ones that are put to
confusion.

> In thee, O LORD, do I put my trust: **let me
> never be put to confusion.** Deliver me in
> thy righteousness, and cause me to escape:
> incline thine ear unto me, and save me.
> Psalms 71:1-2

In contrast, those that trust the Lord can and will
escape confusion. The Lord is not the author of
confusion.

> For God is not the author of confusion, but
> of peace, as in all churches of the saints.
> 1 Corinthians 14:33

How can we save ourselves from this confusion.
We can very simply rely on the Word of God. God
does not contradict Himself and His Word is pure.

> The **words of the LORD are pure
> words**: as silver tried in a furnace of earth,

95

purified seven times. Thou shalt keep them,
O LORD, thou shalt preserve them from this
generation for ever.
Psalms 12:6-7

The Bible not only tells us the Word of God, but it
tells us the Word of God over and over. Take a look
at these phrases used in scripture.

"Thus saith the lord" used 413 times

"It is written" used 80 times

"Word of the Lord" used 255 times

"God said" used 46 times

"Word of God" used 48 times

"Jesus Said" used 65 times

God said it but men repeated it more times than
God said it. And through all of this the Bible does
not contradict itself. We can save ourselves from
confusion by going to the Word of God. Read it for
yourself. Don't take anyone's word for it... trust
only the Word itself. You might be thinking "I can't
read and understand all that stuff." Maybe... but
before you put your trust in the works of men, pray
and ask God to teach you through His Spirit. If you
still have doubts or concerns about the meaning of
scripture, ask another person. When they give you
an answer for your question, don't take it at face
value. Ask them to show you in scripture. "Show
me where it says that." If they cannot show you, or
they have taken scripture out of context... throw it
out until it can be shown to you in scripture in the

proper context. When it comes right down to it... trust the Book.

That trusting of the Bible applies to our internal dialogs also. God will not call a person into something that is in direct opposition to His already written word. God will not ask you to murder someone. He will not bless you in shady business practices. He will not encourage an adulterous relationship. He will NEVER call us into something, or give us instructions that are in contradiction to His written word. Even Jesus used the written words of God in His defense against the guiles of Satan... "It is written..." was His reply to all the temptations Satan placed before Him.

Before God sends someone, He asks them to follow. When He sends them away, He sends them with a purpose and a place. We see this clearly exemplified in the story of Noah.

> But with thee will I establish my covenant; and **thou shalt come into the ark,** thou, and thy sons, and thy wife, and thy sons' wives with thee.
> Genesis 6:18

> And the LORD said unto Noah, **Come thou and all thy house into the ark**; for thee have I seen righteous before me in this generation.
> Genesis 7:1

God calls him into the ark where He is. In essence, "come to Me in the ark". But once the flood has passed and the dry land has appeared, Noah is sent out with a purpose.

And God spake unto Noah, saying, **Go forth of the ark**, thou, and thy wife, and thy sons, and thy sons' wives with thee. Bring forth with thee every living thing that is with thee, of all flesh, both of fowl, and of cattle, and of every creeping thing that creepeth upon the earth; **that they may breed abundantly in the earth, and be fruitful, and multiply upon the earth.**
Genesis 8:15-17

God sent the animals out of the ark with a purpose, and a place to fulfill that purpose. Go out of the ark into the land and populate it. This same instructions were given to Noah and his sons.

And God blessed Noah and his sons, and said unto them, **Be fruitful, and multiply, and replenish the earth.**
Genesis 9:1

The instructions were to go into the earth (the place) and replenish it (the purpose). We can see this same plan in place with Abraham.

Now the LORD had said unto Abram, **Get thee out of thy country**, and from thy kindred, and from thy father's house, unto a land that I will shew thee: And I will make of thee a great nation, and I will bless thee, and make thy name great; and thou shalt be a blessing: And I will bless them that bless thee, and curse him that curseth thee: and in thee shall all families of the earth be blessed.
Genesis 12:1-3

God is telling Abraham, get out of this land and away from your family. Go into the land I will show you (which is the place) and I will make thee a great nation and bless the world through you (the purpose). But before God fulfills that purpose in Abraham He meets him in the way.

> And the LORD appeared unto Abraham, and said, Unto thy seed will I give this land: and there builded he an altar unto the LORD, who appeared unto him.
> Genesis 12:7

God called him into the place that He was, then sent him into the task that He told him of. That task being in a specific land (Canaan) for a specific purpose (blessing the world). Now, the fullness of that purpose would not be fulfilled in Abraham's lifetime, but the purpose was made known to him at the time.

I'd like to share a personal experience of this nature. I was about to enter a fast food restaurant, and it was impressed upon me that I was going to buy someone lunch that day. Believe me when I say that I did not have what you would call "extra" money to do such a thing freely, but the intention was very clear. I went in, there was a lady in front of me about to pay for her meal with a credit card, when the cashier told her the credit card machine was down. I'm thinking this is my chance... this is what I am here for. Her reply was essentially, no problem I have some cash. I was confused... the impression was so clear. I purchased my food and was waiting to be served, when a young man that had obviously been having a hard day came up to the counter. He ordered a very meager meal, and went to pay with a credit card. He was just about in tears when the cashier told him he could not pay with that. Even before he could say he didn't have the cash, I offered to pay. I KNEW that was why I was there. He reluctantly but gratefully accepted. He did not sit with me in the restaurant. Instead, he went and sat with a young lady, either his wife or girlfriend, and they shared their meager meal. I watched as they ate, and their conversation was light and filled with laughter. I am not making any claims to anything other than obedience. But this one action of obedience, prompted by a call with purpose, changed their day. That day could have changed their relationship. The relationship could have changed both of their lives. I don't know the long term results... but I do know that whatever they were, God was in it.

We can see this same calling with purpose again in the life of Abraham in his call to offer Isaac.

> And it came to pass after these things, that God did tempt Abraham, and said unto him, **Abraham**: and he said, **Behold, here I am**. And he said, Take now thy son, thine only son Isaac, whom thou lovest, and get thee into the land of Moriah; and offer him there for a burnt offering upon one of the mountains which I will tell thee of. And Abraham rose up early in the morning, and saddled his ass, and took two of his young men with him, and Isaac his son, and clave the wood for the burnt offering, and rose up, and went unto the place of which God had told him.
> Genesis 22:1-3

God first called Abraham unto Him, then sent him to a specific mount with the specific purpose of offering Isaac. Abraham acted in faith, not knowing what the full outcome would be... but he knew exactly what his part was at the moment. He even brought the wood for the altar.

When Christ was collecting His disciples, without exception, He first told them to "Follow me", calling them unto to Him. Then He sent them out into the world.

> Verily, verily, I say unto thee, When thou wast young, thou girdedst thyself, and walkedst whither thou wouldest: but when thou shalt be old, thou shalt stretch forth thy hands, and another shall gird thee, and carry thee whither thou wouldest not. This spake he, signifying by what death he should glorify God. And when he had spoken this, he saith unto him, **Follow me**.
> John 21:18-19

> The day following Jesus would go forth into Galilee, and findeth Philip, and saith unto him, **Follow me**.
> John 1:43

> Now when Jesus heard these things, he said unto him, Yet lackest thou one thing: sell all that thou hast, and distribute unto the poor, and thou shalt have treasure in heaven: **and come, follow me.**
> Luke 18:22

> And Jesus, walking by the sea of Galilee, saw two brethren, Simon called Peter, and

Andrew his brother, casting a net into the sea: for they were fishers.
And he saith unto them, **Follow me, and I will make you fishers of men.**
Matthew 4:18-19

And as Jesus passed forth from thence, he saw a man, named Matthew, sitting at the receipt of custom: and he saith unto him, **Follow me. And he arose, and followed him.**
Matthew 9:9

Then said Jesus unto his disciples, If any man will come after me, let him deny himself, and **take up his cross, and follow me.**
Matthew 16:24

My sheep hear my voice, and I know them, and they follow me:
John 10:27

He called them unto Him, then sent them into a place, with a purpose.

After these things the Lord appointed other seventy also, and sent them two and two before his face into every city and place, whither he himself would come. Therefore said he unto them, The harvest truly is great, but the labourers are few: pray ye therefore the Lord of the harvest, that he would send forth labourers into his harvest.
Luke 10:1-2

He sent them into the cities where He Himself would go (specific cities) with the purpose of laboring in the harvest. He spends the next 14 or so verses telling them what to expect and what to do and how to do it. He ends His statements with verse 16.

> He that heareth you heareth me; and he that despiseth you despiseth me; and he that despiseth me despiseth him that sent me. And the seventy returned again with joy, saying, Lord, even the devils are subject unto us through thy name.
> Luke 10:16-17

They returned rejoicing over the fact that what He said was true. The point of all this is that God first calls us unto Him to follow Him. Then if He sends us, He sends us with a plan. A place to go, and a purpose when we get there. *If He tells us to go... we are to go with a clear purpose... until that time we are to follow Him.*

> My sheep hear my voice, and I know them, and they follow me: And I give unto them eternal life; and they shall never perish, neither shall any man pluck them out of my hand.
> John 10:27-28

Part 9
Honesty

Something that is implied, but must be addressed is honesty. Throughout this book we have asked several self examination questions concerning the Fruit of the Spirit and the evidence of them in our lives. When we ask these questions, we must be honest with ourselves in the answers. The answers to the questions mean nothing unless they are sincere and truthful.

We are masters at lying. We are born with that nature in us, and some of us can lie so convincingly, that we can even convince ourselves. We must also be careful not to fall into the self-serving trap of comparing ourselves to others. **Others are not our standard.** We can all look at somebody and say "Well, I'm more temperant that that guy... he's just out of control." Or, "At least I am not as bad as she is."

We must also refrain from placing parameters or stipulations on our service to the Lord. Thoughts (or even prayers) like, "I want to love people Lord, and having more money will help me love them better." Is that so? How? Love doesn't cost anything. The Gospel doesn't cost anything. The truth doesn't cost anything... so how can you love someone better with more money? Your answer may be something along the lines of, "Well then I can do more and I won't have to stress as much over the expense." So, the truth is you are stressed over the money because you don't have peace concerning your circumstances. O ye of little faith!

The next thought I would like to share on honesty is... doing well in one area does not "balance out" doing poorly in other areas. "I don't have to be as self controlled, because I am generous in helping others." This is a lie. "I can be harsh in the truth, because it shows that I am passionate about the Word of God." This is a false belief.

Certainly, there are areas where we will find it easier to grow and maintain ourselves. We all have differing personalities and strengths. But the real truth of the matter is, when we are examining ourselves, we are not comparing ourselves to others. We may be in a balance, but it is God's set of scales. Just as it tells us in Job...

> Doth not he see my ways, and count all my steps? If I have walked with vanity, or if my foot hath hasted to deceit; Let me be weighed in an even balance, that **God may know mine integrity.**
> Job 31:4-6

The honesty we seek is between ourselves and God. And God has a few things to say about the balance.

> A **false balance is abomination** to the LORD: but **a just weight is his delight.**
> Proverbs 11:1

> A just weight and balance are the LORD'S: **all the weights of the bag are his work.**
> Proverbs 16:11

God despises the false balance, but He smiles upon the just weight. And the just weights can only be found in Him. When we are assessing our honesty in the asking of these questions, we cannot concern ourselves with whether or not our moms think we are honest, or our spouses think we are honest, or if our Pastor thinks we are honest. Does God know that I am being honest? His is the only opinion that truly matters. And no matter how convincingly we may be able to fool others, or even ourselves, God knows the whole truth.

> Then hear thou from heaven thy dwelling place, and forgive, and render unto every man according unto all his ways, whose heart thou knowest; (**for thou only knowest the hearts of the children of men:**)
> 2 Chronicles 6:30

> Correction is grievous unto him that forsaketh the way: and he that hateth reproof shall die. Hell and destruction are before the LORD: **how much more then the hearts of the children of men?**
> Proverbs 15:10-11

The Lord sees into the true intentions of the hearts of men. He is not concerned with the outward man. He is not looking at what we do as much as why we do it. And He sees everything.

This should actually be a comforting thing for us. If He has an intimate detailed knowledge of our thoughts and doings, then when we come to Him to ask forgiveness or make supplication... we need not hold anything back. We can be fully open and honest with Him who knows it all already. He sees into the hearts, the intentions of men, and not just the outward appearances.

The fining pot is for silver, and the furnace for gold: but the LORD trieth the hearts.
Proverbs 17:3

It is the Lord that puts us in the balance, and it is by His standard that we are tried. It is by His just weight that our intentions are balanced. These last few verses from 1 Thessalonians should help set things straight.

> For our exhortation was not of deceit, nor of uncleanness, nor in guile: But as we were allowed of God to be put in trust with the gospel, **even so we speak; not as pleasing men, but God,** which trieth our hearts. For neither at any time used we flattering words, as ye know, nor a cloke of covetousness; God is witness: Nor of men sought we glory, neither of you, nor yet of others, when we might have been burdensome, as the apostles of Christ.
> 1 Thessalonians 2:3-6

They spoke to please God, not men. They threw off the cloak of covetousness (which could mean the desire to be self-serving), and spoke the words of God. And who was their witness that they had done this... God himself.

What a powerful instrument of God we could be if we would learn to apply these simple yet life changing principles set forth in God's Fruit of the Spirit.

Part 10
Summary

What we have seen through this study is that God's Spirit can be evidenced in us. In our works, which bare the fruit of the Gospel, and in our daily walk in the form of the Fruit of that Spirit. When we ask ourselves these questions concerning the evidence of the fruit in our lives, we can *know* if we are walking in the Spirit of God. We can take these principles set forth by the Fruit of the Spirit and know if we are conducting ourselves in a way that will produce that fruit in our lives and be pleasing to God. The fruit that we produce is for others, not for ourselves.

First and foremost, all that we do should be driven by God's love abiding in us. That is the primary focus of all that we do, and through **love** we satisfy all the law. The various facets of that love can be seen in the other Fruit of the Spirit.

In times of peace and plenty, we should have **joy** in the Lord and praise Him. We should be able to share in the joy of others when they are blessed and delivered. In times of struggle, oppression and fear, we should have **peace**, knowing He is there with us and will never forsake us.

In our interactions with the hardhearted and contentious, we should have an attitude of **longsuffering**. Consider and try to emulate the longsuffering the Lord has towards us. In our dealings with the brokenhearted and downtrodden, we should have an attitude of **gentleness**, never a spirit of judgment or condemnation.

Our actions toward others should always be done in **goodness** to all people, never in spite or anger.

And our actions in response to God and what He has asked of us in His Word should be founded on unwavering **faith**.

In our dealings with those that call themselves Children of God, we ought to have a Spirit of **meekness** which we have seen is passion for the Word of God and earnest intercession for the brother or sister that has strayed. And in dealing with our own rebellious flesh, we must have a Spirit of **temperance**, which is not just control, but mastery over that which is in opposition to God.

If any other fruit are being produced in our hearts or minds, or worse yet being perceived by others, then our actions and thoughts are not following after the Fruit of the Spirit of God. We are not producing, as His children, what God would have us produce.

> For a good tree bringeth not forth corrupt fruit; neither doth a corrupt tree bring forth good fruit.
> Luke 6:43

It is my sincere prayer that anyone who reads this book would come to that place of honesty with God, and see what kind of change can be wrought in their lives. Also, that they would seek diligently to manifest these Fruit of the Spirit in their lives; seek them all, not just the ones they are good at, and see how God can truly change their lives and touch the lives around them.

I leave this with you in the name of Jesus Christ, Peace and God Bless You!